When Heaven Touched Filey

This is an account, based on historical facts, of the remarkable events which started in March 1823 and which brought about long lasting transformation in the lives of many of the small fishing community of Filey.

This Yorkshire village became internationally known as a place which had received a significant and privileged visitation.

The content of this work is based on actual facts and is true to the best of my knowledge. I consider that I have not so much written this work, as rather that I have compiled pieces of work from many different sources and put all the relevant material together into one publication. I have attempted to attribute each source that I have used with the acknowledgement in the bibliography at the end of the book. Any acknowledgements that I have missed are purely accidental and not intentional and I apologise if that is the case. AB.

ISBN 978-1-90446-47-7

When Heaven Touched Filey.

Published and printed by
Quacks Books
7 Grape Lane
Petergate
York YO1 7HU

Acknowledgements

In writing this account, I am indebted to the staff of both Filey and Scarborough public libraries for the assistance that has been given. I greatly appreciate the help given by the staff of the Crimlisk Fisher Archives at Filey Town Council Offices who also supplied some of the documents for use. Filey Museum has generously made available many photographs and has kindly given permission for their use.

My heartfelt thanks go to the many friends who have patiently read the various draft stages of this publication and have suggested changes, improvements and additions. I am extremely grateful to have such friends willing to give their time and thoughts to do this without any complaining and just viewing it as a labour of love! I want to say a huge 'thank you' to Jenny H, Ruth B, Sally D, Kate C, Chris and Margaret W, Richard and Judith A, Mike D. Without their help and encouragement this account would probably not have seen the light of day. AB.

Preface

Before you turn to the next page will you pause and ask yourself the question: - "Could I possibly imagine feeling confident enough to walk down a darkened street of my town (or any town) by myself at midnight?"

Can I picture a place where there is no danger of violence from rowdy or drunken behaviour in the streets?

The town is such that children can go safely to school on their own and the elderly have no need to fear for their own personal safety.

Try to picture a scene where there is no need to lock the door of your house when going out because there is no theft, and when picking up a newspaper, reading only good news stories.

The magistrates' courts are virtually empty because of the lack of cases to hear.

Imagine, if you can, a place where people are genuinely caring for each other and giving support when needed.
Can you picture such a scene?

Does all this sound like some unattainable fantasy, something which is highly unlikely, unrealistic and even impossible? Too good to be true?

Yet something like this actually became a reality in Filey one hundred and ninety years ago..........

Something happened to bring about a radical change in the community's attitudes and values. The following account is a record of actual events which happened in Filey. The pivotal moment in time was 23rd March 1823. This was the watershed point, the defining moment, which was later to be seen to have separated two distinct ways of the community's life.

The consequences which followed from that date were deep, profound and long lasting. The changes to the life of the community, and the on-going effects, were still being felt at the turn of the 20th century.

The remarkable transformation in the lives of the small fishing community of Filey was so newsworthy, so unlikely and so unexpected that written reports reverberated across the ocean to the USA and beyond.

Filey became known as a place that had received especial favour, a place which had experienced an unusual and unexpected blessing.

That something extraordinary happened cannot be doubted.

There is overwhelming evidence to this and much of this still remains and speaks to us today.

There are at least six pieces of evidence which survive that bear witness to the events of that time.

They are: -

1) A large brick building in Union Street Filey,
2) A derelict windmill on the approach to Filey,
3) The Filey Fishermen's Choir,
4) Records in Filey Museum and Filey Town Archives,
5) Various written accounts in the Scarborough Public Library,
6) Several books, most notably "Praying Johnny" the biography of Johnny Oxtoby by Rev George Shaw.

The fact that so much evidence still remains from what became known as "The Filey Revival" has greatly helped in the research for this publication. Also the evidence reminds us today of what a powerful impact the events made upon the community of that time and how the resulting consequences continued to reverberate down the next several generations.

Yet this is only one of the stories that could have been told. Similar stories could also be recounted of the events which profoundly changed the lives of many people of Scarborough, Bridlington and Driffield and the surrounding villages during the same period.

The purpose of producing this account is threefold:-
1) To examine what it was that actually happened.

2) It is an attempt to stand back and appreciate how deeply the effects were felt by many of the people of Filey from 1823

onwards and what the consequences were.

3) That by bringing together the various factors into one account, a more complete record can be kept for posterity.

The account is based on recorded facts of what actually took place. It records that a great transformation did actually take place in the lives of many of the Filey people of that time and also in the lives of their descendants.

Hopefully this will encourage us of the 21st Century to be able to appreciate that there can still be hope and that changes in our communities are possible. The seemingly continuing spiralling down of standards and values of society are not necessarily inevitable.

Alan Botterill.

February 2013.

Contents

Chapters

Note: for numbers in parenthesis please refer to the Bibliography.

Illustrations

CHAPTER 1:
Filey and Fishing.

Probably no part of England's east coast is more picturesque than Filey Bay.

To the south are the high chalk cliffs of Flamborough Head, and to the north is the much lower Filey Brigg extending for about a mile out into the sea. Between the two, like the crusty end of a generously cut piece of apple pie, is the long arc which makes up the coastline of Filey Bay. On the edge of this, Filey town nestles closely into the cliffs.

This location, together with seven miles of clean, sandy beach, makes for an idyllic picture. It is understandably popular with the many holiday makers who flock here during the summer months. It is highly regarded and is truly a "bonny spot".
Since the arrival of the railway to Filey in 1846/7, tourism has continued to grow until now the holiday trade has become the most important element in the town's economy. Fishing has still a part in Filey's life, but its former premier position has been overtaken by the growth of tourism.

Contrast this with the Filey of the early 19th century and we find a very different picture. Where today the population of Filey is around 6500, in the census of 1821 it was only 773. Then it was only a fair sized village. It was described as "one short row of cottages waiting for visitors who never came". (1)

Filey was well known as a large and important fishing port. There was a significant international export trade, some of the salted fish, and dried skate wings in particular, being shipped to Portugal. Then, as always has been the case, fishing was uncertain and unpredictable, especially so before the age of steam and mechanical power.

With sail, the livelihood of Filey was largely dependant on the wind. The strength and direction of the wind made the difference between going out to fish or not. It was the wind which made the difference between a potentially successful trip with a good catch of fish, or possible shipwreck and disaster.

In winter, fishing was from cobles (local fishing boats). Each coble usually had twelve lines each having about 160 hooks. Huge quantities of bait were needed for the lines to be baited, and it was a continual tread-mill of hard work to keep them supplied. It was the women and strong girls who were expected to gather bait for the fishing lines. The bait was commonly shellfish gathered locally, frequently limpets known locally as "flithers", and also mussels.

Waste fish was also used, some of it being imported from other nearby fishing ports. The hooks had to be baited and this also required a lot of effort as it took one man about an hour and a half to bait one line. For the twelve lines it took about eighteen man-hours just to bait the lines for one coble.

Life was hard for all in the fishing community, both for men and women. But it was especially tough for the women as their work involved gathering the bait. This took long hours of hard, back-breaking work, and in all weathers. This was particularly demanding for the women who had also to maintain the family home. Added to this was the constant anxiety as they waited for their men to come back from their hazardous work at sea.

It is not easy for us today to realise the dangers that the fishermen of the 19th Century faced, which they regarded as normal. This was especially so on the East Coast of Yorkshire.

Flamborough Head and Filey Brigg were welcome sights for many crews who needed to have their position at sea confirmed, but they were also terrifying sights when gale force winds and high seas were sweeping them towards the rocky shore to their vessel's destruction and their likely deaths. Both Flamborough Head and Filey Brigg claimed many vessels. Shipwreck was common-place.

There was an old seamen's rhyme which sounded a warning of the dangers of the rocky headlands of the Yorkshire coast:-

"Flamborough head you must pass by,
Filey Brigg you must not come nigh,
Scarborough Castle stands over the sea,
And Whitby rocks lie northerly." (2)

Accurate records for the wrecks of the 17th/18th/19th centuries are sketchy and almost certainly incomplete. In one account we read that *"many ships wrecked in Filey Bay during the great storm of November 1696. In 1740 nine large ships were lost in Filey Bay along with two thirds of their crew. In 1823, three fishing vessels wrecked in Filey Bay – three crew members drowned. In 1869, eight hundred and thirty eight ships wrecked off the East Coast."* (3) Many other examples could be listed.

It is estimated that 2000 seamen were lost at sea off the coast of the British Isles each year during the period 17th/18th and 19th centuries. *The average life expectancy of seamen was only 45 years.*(4) Many vessels were poorly maintained and often barely seaworthy. There were little or no regulatory powers in place to ensure greater safety. Also it was widely accepted that the drunken state of many of the crews, of vessels laden with coal and other goods, was often a contributory factor for poor seamanship which led to a vessel's loss.

We need to keep in mind that shipwrecks were so frequently occurring that many went unrecorded. They were comparable in "news-worthiness" to present day road accidents, and where no lives were lost, they had little news value and so went virtually unrecorded.

The name *Filey* was synonymous with fishing. Essentially it was a fishing village. The community's life revolved around fishing and virtually the whole local economy depended upon it. At Filey several families are recognised as "old Filey fishing families". Records show the fishing connection to families going back beyond five generations with the names such as Cammish, Haxby, Jenkinson and several others, all of them closely involved with fishing.

Fishing was important to Filey. The industry supplied employment for many at Filey. (courtesy Filey Museum)

The author was able to meet with Ben Jenkinson in February 2013 to learn more about the life of Filey fishermen and their families. It was the earlier generations of the Jenkinson family who in the 1820's were some of the key people in the work of the Primitive Methodists in Filey.

Ben, who has spent his whole life involved in the fishing industry, said that there was always a great disparity in incomes between families, some were always in poverty and there were other families who fared much better.

Several reasons were responsible, one being the skill of the men at catching fish; some were more skilled than others and regularly caught more fish. But the willingness to put out to sea was also a factor. Some were willing to go out in marginally unsafe sea and weather conditions. Others were not. It was a balance between risk and reward. The reward for taking more risk was landing a catch for the market when less fish was available and so prices were likely to be higher. There would be less competition for the buyers to choose from.

There was a very real risk of loss of life for all those working on the sea. But the risk to fishermen was greater because their family's livelihoods were at stake. Fish was vital to their families' economy. If they did not catch fish, then their family didn't eat.

Accidents could, and did, happen at any time without warning. Weather could change very quickly, misjudgement of situations, and numerous other factors, all could play a part in causing accidents. This was considered to be just part of the normal everyday run- of- the- mill risk which went with this way of life.

But when accidents happened at sea they were frequently fatal. There are plenty of headstones in St Oswald's Churchyard at Filey to confirm this, with 'drowned' and 'lost at sea', being the inscriptions for many men and boys of all ages who did not return to shore alive.

Just a short walk in the Churchyard and you encounter these gravestones:-

Matthew Jenkinson- aged 31-drowned-3rd Jly 1849,

William Jenkinson-aged 32-drowned at sea-2nd Nov-1861,

Mathew Jenkinson-aged 31-drowned in Filey Bay 1st Dec1863,

George Jenkinson-aged 27-drowned near Filey Brigg-16th Jan 1874,

Ross Jenkinson-aged 38 -lost at sea-29th Oct 1888, aged 38

George Jenkinson-aged 20-lost at sea in Filey Bay-14th Dec 1896,

Edmond Ross Jenkinson -aged 30-lost at sea-28th April 1892.

John R Jenkinson- born 1862   } all drowned in the
Robert Jenkinson- born 1890   } "Research" Disaster
George F B Jenkinson- born 1897 } 25/11/1925

There are very many other similar memorials in the Churchyard which could be added to this list. Other Filey fishing families have similar headstones recording past tragedies.

Fish came onto the table at a much greater cost than merely the financial outlay.

On the Yorkshire coast each fishing community had its own individual pattern of heavy duty woollen jumper or 'gansey' for the men to wear. The Filey patterned ganseys were, and still are, knitted locally. Because of the individual pattern of these garments it was possible to identify straight away which place the person belonged to. This enabled the drowned fishermen's bodies to be returned home for identification and burial.

But frequently the drowned men's bodies were never recovered. And because there was often no information of the overdue fishing vessel's loss, it was not possible to bring closure to the probable loss of someone's loved one. They *may* somehow have managed to survive and be able to come home late. This hope gave rise to the practice of fishing families in Filey of never locking their house doors, even at night, just in case *they* might come back home sometime. This was still the custom in the 1950's.

The fishermen's lives were filled with hard work, danger and uncertainty. There was always the uncertainty of income as the size and sale value of the catch was always unpredictable.

Charles Kingsley wrote:-

> "For men must work and women must weep
>
> And there's little to earn and many to keep"

This was particularly true for the fishing community in the early 19th century.

CHAPTER 2 :
Filey's Notoriety.

In the early 19th century Filey was well known throughout the local area. There was a reputation attached to the town, and it was one of notoriety.

Filey was notorious for "vice and wickedness of every description." (1)

Exactly what the moral state of Filey was cannot be completely known, but by having 'a reputation' it clearly shows that the community had sunk to a fairly low level of morality even by the standards of that time. By being "noted for vice and wickedness" shows that Filey was more of an unsavoury place than the other towns of the locality.

A common sign outside public houses throughout England was "Drunk for a penny, dead drunk for two pence, straw to lie on."

We may think that the permissive society of Britain in the early 21st century has sunk to previously unplumbed depths. Yet the 18th and early 19th century theatre and much of the literature of that period would still be classed as pornographic today.(2)

Throughout England at this time, sports such as bear and bull-baiting, cock-fighting, with much gambling, was widespread and was both carnal and brutal. Pugilism, bare-fist fighting, was savage and murderous – and even women took part.

Violence was also rampant, both on and off the streets. Law enforcement was haphazard and largely ineffective. Polygamy, promiscuity and extreme depraved behaviour were not considered wrong, sinful or even unusual. Depravity in all its forms appears to have been widespread.

John Wesley wrote "...the obscenity of the stage – that stink of all corruption". ".......gangs of drunken ruffians paraded the streets and subjected women to nameless outrages. The constables shared the drunken habits of the time and were mainly corrupt." (3)

On pay day the men frequently took their wages straight into the ale-houses rather than into their homes. Their drunken behaviour, which frequently led to household violence, together with the loss of their wages caused much widespread hardship to their families.

The writer Silvester Horne in "Popular History of the Free Churches" wrote "The whole population of England seemed to be given over to an orgy of drunkenness which made the very name of Englishmen to stink in the nostrils of other nations."

When Wesley wrote about the moral state of England in 1739, he described society as it was at that time. During the next several decades much of England changed as he and others travelled the country and established what was to become the Methodist Church. This had a great reforming influence nationally. It is highly likely that Britain avoided being plunged into a similar

11

revolution to that which overwhelmed France because of the reforming work of the early Methodists.

The Wesleyan Methodist Church at Filey was weak, with only 15 members in 1823, and was making little progress in affecting the community. H B Kendall's report describes the state of the Methodist Church as "struggling for existence" and of the Anglican Church, he wrote "the influence of the Anglican Church was almost a negative quantity.......St Oswald's may as well have been in another world as in another Riding". (4) (At that time St Oswald's, the Anglican Church building, was in the North Riding, and the rest of Filey was in East Riding. The boundary ran through the valley known as 'Church Ravine' which separated the two.)

H B Kendall continued:-"In Filey, there was plenty of superstition..... but of real religion there was little enough. The fishermen were blasphemous and addicted to alcohol---- drunkenness, cock-fighting and card playing were common-place. The Sabbath was disregarded, if anything it was the busiest day of the week."

While there was little Christian influence on the fishing community, the same cannot be said for superstition. It had a strong hold on the people's behaviour in everyday life. For example, if you tried to buy eggs after sunset you would bring very bad luck on the person you tried to buy them from. Also to hear the words 'pig' and 'rabbit' were extremely unlucky. The very mention of either name was enough to prevent a man going to sea that day, yet it was considered acceptable to substitute the words "grunter" and "bunny"!

The mere sight of a grey horse was certain to influence the size of catch. If a grey horse was seen, then the catch would be very small. It would hardly be worth the while. Whistling was considered to be very dangerous. It was likely to whistle up a gale and endanger everyone in that sea area.

One of the strangest superstitions was the belief that it was necessary to gather horse-drawn carts and wagons and form a funnel shaped grouping on top of the cliffs after the herring fishing fleet had put to sea. This was considered essential for a good catch of herring. The wagons and carts had to remain in position for several days. It was believed this would ensure big catches of herring. (5)

These and other superstitions had a powerful controlling influence on the people's lives. Many local customs were kept, all involving heavy drinking sessions, be it weddings, funerals or celebrating the annual calendar events of 'Carlin Sunday', Easter or Christmas. The one thing they had in common was a reason to be able to drink alcohol to excess.(6) It would seem that 'Binge' drinking is not just a 21st Century problem!

With the hazardous and uncertain way of life for the

fishermen, the restrictive hold of superstition and no real faith in God – all this must have given a sense of helplessness and resignation to an almost inevitable impending disaster. All these ingredients, together with the reputation of "every kind of wickedness", made Filey a parlous and desperately dismal place, a place to avoid, for in the local parlance Filey "was a rum spot".

Various visiting preachers had come to the place to attempt to speak about the Gospel to the folk there but they hadn't been given a hearing. They had always either been roughed up or shouted down and sometimes both at the same time. On one famous occasion the preacher was pelted with dried salted fish and driven out of the place with bruises to remind him of his visit! At another time a bunch of pigs was turned loose in amongst the few people who were in a church meeting. This quickly brought that gathering to an end!

This was the situation of Filey at the beginning of the year 1823, but it was soon to be transformed, for by the end of that year, such profound changes had taken place that the lives of many of the residents were completely changed for ever.

The news of these events was to echo across the Atlantic Ocean to the United States and beyond. The name of Filey was to become known as a place which had received special Divine favour as the events were recorded for posterity. The pivotal moment was the 23rd of March 1823.

CHAPTER 3:
"Cometh the Hour, Cometh the Man."

On to this stage stepped John Oxtoby. He was a countryman, a man of the soil, from a farming background, being born in 1767 at Little Givendale, near Pocklington. His father had a small farm which was lost soon after John was born. John hadn't any of the privileges of wealth, position or schooling beyond only the basic village school education to the normal leaving age of 13 or 14. He started to work as a labourer on the surrounding farms as soon as he left school.

All those who worked on the land were used to long days. For six days of the week the day started in the stables at 5 a.m. feeding, grooming and mucking-out the horses. Breakfast was at 6 a.m. Work started with horses being already harnessed for work by 7 a.m. The day finished usually at 6 p.m. but during harvest time it was often much later. Except for the feeding and basic care of livestock, Sunday was the much valued, and much needed, day of rest!

This would be the pattern of John's life for the next 30 years.

During this time he became a regular member of the local church. He was so consistent that whenever he was missing from church through illness, his absence was noticed and people wondered what had stopped him from being there.

In 1804 at the age of 37, John was becoming dissatisfied with just "attending" church. He was just an ordinary, hard working man who wasn't given over to wild living. But he had a feeling within him that there had to be more to life than that which he was experiencing.

But he didn't know what it, "the more" was, or how to find "it". It was like having an inner itch which couldn't be scratched.

Then, in that same year, he heard a Methodist preacher speak on "Saving Faith". This enabled him to take the step that he had been looking for but hadn't been able to find. He became a Christian, and as the Bible says, he was "born again" (1) and he knew that what he had been looking for he had found!

He was able to come to trust Jesus Christ as his Lord and Saviour.

This changed his whole outlook. From then on he devoted his life to sharing his faith with whoever would listen. John became a member of the Wesleyan Methodist church and soon started visiting everyone in the village of Warter. Every home was visited and every family prayed for. For a while he met with opposition but at length his visits were more than welcomed.

He is described as not being too concerned about fashionable clothes. He dressed like a farmer from the generation before, usually wearing a chocolate coloured neckerchief, a broad brimmed hat, a 'flitch of bacon' coat, close fitting knee-breeches, hob-nailed boots, and his hair combed down to his eyebrows. He was unmarried, of average height, had a well built frame, brown eyes and light brown hair.

In 1818 he left the Wesleyans and joined the Primitive Methodists "because they had a stronger faith and were harder working in saving souls."

"The Prims", as the Primitive Methodists were called, were also affectionately known as "Ranters" because of their very noisy meetings, especially their lively, loud singing! They were a group which separated from the Wesleyan Methodists.

To John, God and the devil, good and evil, heaven and hell were not abstract concepts but vivid realities. He became an itinerant local preacher, speaking wherever he was invited. He rejoiced in being 'God-made' and not a school or college made preacher.

He had a great dislike for written sermons which he called "paper pellets." His speech was broad Yorkshire, natural and unpretentious.

Good lungs, graphic descriptive power, real faith and the gift of prayer; these were the qualifications that the ordinary people could understand and appreciate, and John had them in abundance. Such was his power in prayer that he was widely known as "Praying Johnny" because his prayers were answered so frequently and so immediately.

Primitive Methodist friends from Bridlington had tried again and again to start a work in Filey. They had spoken in streets, barns and a variety of sheds but every time they had been mobbed, shouted down and pelted out of the place. They remembered the occasion when some pigs were driven amongst the congregation while they were trying to hold a meeting.(2)

Early in 1823 in Bridlington, a planning meeting for the Church's work was under way. The subject of Filey was raised. Was it worth continuing with? Should Filey be given up and the resources used more profitably elsewhere? Should Filey be considered a lost cause and the Primitive Methodist Church withdraw from that Godless place?

When Johnny was asked for his opinion he replied "The Lord has a great work to do in Filey, send me. I'll live on taties (potatoes) and sleep on a board afooare (before) it shall be given up." The meeting decided to give Filey another chance and agreed that Johnny at the age of fifty six should go to Filey. Being so active and fit at Johnny's age was in itself unusual. At this time, the early 19th Century, anyone in their mid-fifties was considered well on in years.

He remained unmarried all his life. This allowed him to travel at short notice without domestic considerations restricting his work. He could be available to go where needed and he believed he was needed at Filey.

The following Sunday in mid-March 1823, Johnny was on the way to Filey. He met an acquaintance on the way to Filey and on discovering Johnny's mission, he said "It's a forlorn hope, Johnny, you had better go back." Johnny was adamant "I'm gooin to Filey, where the Lord is gooin to revive his work."

CHAPTER 4:
Johnny Oxtoby arrives at Filey.

As Johnny continued on his way, he eventually came to Muston Mill Hill on the approach to Filey. Suddenly a view of Filey burst upon him.
He was so filled with an urgency to pray for the place and for the success of his mission that he immediately fell on his knees and started to pray.

There was good reason why he was known as "Praying Johnny". It was a habit that he had developed over many years. He had seen many answers to his prayers. He believed that God, his heavenly Father, wanted him to pray and wanted to answer the prayer of faith. The bible says that "the prayer of a righteous man is powerful and effective". (1) This had certainly been Johnny's personal experience.
He had become used to spending hours in prayer speaking to his heavenly Father. His often heard advice was "If you will only pray and believe, you will see great things, only pray and believe!"

So he started to pray behind the roadside hedge for Filey and for the success of his mission. He continued on his knees for "several hours", weeping and pleading. He must have been noisy, for the neighbouring miller working at the nearby windmill heard the commotion and went to see what was happening. What he heard were not respectable, dignified, quiet, "churchy" prayers! This was different. There was a guts-honest reality and desperation in this man's prayers. For him, it had to be real and sincere and it involved his whole person.

The remains of the windmill on Mill Hill on the approach to Filey where Johnny Oxtoby prayed for Filey.

The miller stopped to listen in astonishment. He heard Johnny saying: "Thou moant mak a feal o me! Thou moant mak a feal o me! (You mustn't make a fool of me) I told them at Bollitton (Burlington, now Bridlington) that Thou was goin' to revive Thy work, and Thou must deah (do) so, or I shall nivver be able to show my face amang em aggen (among them again), and then what will the people say about praying and believing?"

He continued to pray, rolling backwards and forwards on the ground, then onto his knees, and back again onto the ground. This went on for several hours, but he wouldn't give up.

At length he believed that his prayers had been heard and had been answered. He felt a release from further prayer, rest filled his soul, and he jumped up shouting "It is done Lord. It is done. Filey is takken (taken). Filey is takken! Glory, Filey is takken!" He knew that a change had taken place! And what a change it was!

Johnny continued on into Filey. As he entered the place, and going down King Street (now Queen Street), he started singing the hymn "Turn to the Lord and seek Salvation". A crowd of fishermen gathered round to listen. Johnny then started to speak to them. He spoke with such an unusual power and authority that the people listened intently. He was carrying a message different from anything that the people had heard before.

King Street Filey circa 1820.

*King Street/Queenstreet Filey circa 1900, little changed from the 1820's.
The area was largely demolished and redeveloped in mid-1970's. (Courtesy
Filey Museum)*

He was bringing a message of good news. It was a message of hope. There *was* an alternative to their present situation. Johnny Oxtoby was carrying the spiritual characteristics of love, joy, peace, patience, faithfulness and self-control. (2)

As he spoke a dramatic effect took place. The systems of two different worlds collided. Light flooded into darkness. Spiritual awareness dispelled ignorance. Faith pushed back fear. God awareness flooded through godlessness. Hope replaced resignation. Superstition lost its power.

For the people, it was a spiritual encounter which was beyond logic, reason, expectation or any previous experience. Johnny's words seemed to pierce to the very centre of the listeners hearts. People wept, others trembled and more than a *dozen* fell on to their knees and cried aloud for mercy and--- amazingly---found it.(3)

Tough, hardened, feet-on-the-ground, worldly-wise fishermen, these were the ones who were now so convicted of their need to change their lives and their behaviour that they were on their knees weeping! This was the same community which had ridiculed and driven out previous preachers.

Whenever Johnny addressed the assembled crowds he spoke in his ordinary broad Yorkshire accent, but with unusual power. His addresses were not cleverly constructed intellectual sermons. He was not that kind of man. He was a man of the soil, a farm labourer. His speech was simple and easily understood but it had the capacity to get right through to the inmost part of a person. His speech was empowered with "power from on high" (4).

When he spoke, his words pierced the hearts of those listening and many recognised that they needed to respond to the good news of the Gospel message. Those who did accept the gospel message and receive Jesus Christ as their Saviour found a deep peace that they hadn't previously known. Not all responded positively, but many did.

After Johnny Oxtoby had spoken in King Street, he stayed that night in the house of Willy Jenk who lived at the top of Spring Row just off from King street. He continued to stay for a while in Filey, visiting house to house during the day and holding meetings during the evenings.

Over the next several days a large number of people's lives were seen to change. Many found that their old habits and addictions of a lifetime were broken, their behaviour and their lives being totally transformed. This was particularly true for those who were heavily addicted of alcohol, and this at a time when drinking to excess was commonplace.

Soon there was a marked decrease in drunken behaviour

as alcohol dependency was broken and people were able to give up drinking to excess. This was apparent to all and was confirmed in the words of the vicar of Filey, Rev T Jackson who wrote that he had not seen a drunken fisherman in the whole of the 50 years (after 1823) that he lived at Filey. (5) Similarly Rev C Kendall wrote regarding Filey, "Drunkenness is little known.......... intemperance, happily, is a rare occurrence" (5)

In the 21st Century many of us know and can appreciate how difficult it is to break any addiction, be it sexual lust, smoking, drinking to excess, eating to excess or even the using of "recreational" drugs.

Yet in 1823 we see that in this community, many households were permanently set free from alcohol dependency. The addiction was broken virtually immediately and permanently! This is quite remarkable.

Perhaps at this point we need to suspend the narrative to ask the question: - What was it that was happening on that street in Filey when Johnny Oxtoby spoke that could have had such profound effects upon those listening? Can it be explained?

Could it be a speaker appealing to people's emotions and whipping up hysteria?

It sounds highly unlikely, bearing in mind the nature of his audience. Loss of self-control would be the last thing these tough Yorkshiremen would want. They would not want to lose their dignity, particularly in front of those who knew them so well! Definitely not showing their tears! Certainly they would not want to show weakness and lose their credibility in front of either their workmates or the other folks they knew! Surely they would sooner just walk away with their true feelings tightly bottled up and under their control.

Could the speaker have manipulated the listeners with clever words?

This seems unlikely when we know Oxtoby's background, having little education or much training at public speaking. He was known as having "unexceptional" and "unremarkable" mental abilities. Common sense tells us that it had to be something else.

Was it just an aberration? An unexplainable event?

Or is just possible that what was happening could have been the same as that which has occurred on numerous occasions throughout history in many different parts of the world?

The first recorded instance of something like this was in the year 33AD in Jerusalem (6). Since then, throughout history, many similar events have taken place, for example, in Ireland in 1859-60, in Wales 1904-05, in Scotland 1839-41, in North Uist 1957-58 and are now currently taking place in China in the 21st Century. All these have had the same three basic characteristics, the people becoming acutely aware of the holiness of God, a deep compulsion for them to get their lives right with God, and a feeling of responsibility to care for other people.

This event at Filey, this "happening", bears all the hallmarks of a classic heavenly intervention which is sometimes called "a revival", "an outpouring" or "an awakening". Whenever a revival move of God occurs it is always powerful and gives people a great compulsion to get their lives right with God. When revival happens, it is always first birthed in heaven because it is of divine origin.

This revival, at Filey although highly unusual, was not without precedence in England. Perhaps we need reminding that the Methodist Church movement itself was formed from revival activity throughout England in the 18th century which was on a massive scale during the time of the ministry of John Wesley. These occasions of revival activity occur when divine power is released from heaven to touch a group of people. Some other examples of this happening are listed at the end of this publication.

However disturbing it may seem to us of today, the evidence of the eye-witnesses, and their changed lives, all overwhelmingly support the conclusion that it was a Spiritual Revival in Filey that had broken out. The events at Filey bear all the hallmarks of a move of God.

No other explanation seems to satisfactorily fit the facts.

Heaven had touched Filey.

While Johnny Oxtoby was in Filey, the transformation of the community continued to develop and grow. Many people were affected, many ordinary people becoming believers – the very people who had previously dismissed all other Christian contacts with great hostility. The community, with such notoriety due to its bad reputation, was now recognised as being a place of great blessing because of the events of March 1823, the time when Heaven touched Filey.

CHAPTER 5 :
Blazing Faith and Transformed People.

One spark can start a forest fire. Once the fire is under way, the resultant inferno is no longer reliant upon the spark. 'Revival' is very much like that. John Oxtoby was the catalyst through which Divine Power was released. Once burning, the revival ran through the Filey community, changing many people's lives. This changed their outlook, their hopes, their behaviour and their beliefs.

In short, their lives were transformed as they found faith in God. Their faith was not dependent upon Johnny Oxtoby or any other person. Their faith was a personal faith. They had found faith in their Lord who they now knew loved and cared for them. So profound were their experiences that they could now no longer condone their previously normal and accepted standard of behaviour. For many, their lives were totally transformed.

This could be seen through the change of behaviour patterns and activities which started to take place immediately after Oxtoby had brought the Gospel to Filey. He spent time with the people teaching the new Christians the necessity of seeking to share with others those blessings that they themselves had received.

But Johnny Oxtoby was more than just a gifted

preacher.

Above all Johnny was widely known for his ability to pray effectively and get answers to his praying! His often repeated advice was- "Only pray and believe, pray and believe and you will see great things!" That was why he was affectionately nicknamed "Praying Johnny".

Widespread changes started taking place in the community:-

People were healed supernaturally through prayer.
Johnny Oxtoby had frequently prayed in other locations for people to receive healing and he had seen many people completely healed. It is recorded by Rev George Shaw that at Filey also some people were healed through prayer. Many were healed of their alcohol addictions. Others were healed of diseases.

On one occasion, in the evening, when Oxtoby went to a house to preach he saw that there was a child who had "an affliction", some form of paralyses, a condition which prevented the child being able to walk or even stand. He prayed for the child's condition to be healed. There was great rejoicing when next day the youngster was able to get up from the bed, walk unaided and then was able to play around the house with all symptoms totally absent. The child made a full recovery to health.

This was considered a great miracle and caused a huge degree of amazement and comment.

Mrs Gordon was one of the earliest to be healed supernaturally. In her earlier years she had lived in Ceylon (Sri Lanka), having had a good education and with her husband was seen as being part of "the best of society" of Ceylon. Unfortunately she fell dangerously ill in Ceylon and her doctor strongly advised a return to England. He recommended her to settle at an English seaside town because of her dangerous state of health. Soon after she arrived to live in Filey, more misfortune struck when the jewel of her life, her own child, tragically died.

In her already weakened state Mrs Gordon slipped into a deep depression of grief. It was at this point in her life that Johnny Oxtoby entered Filey with his message of love and healing. Mrs Gordon's husband encouraged her to go and listen to him preach: - "Jane, there is a man called Praying Johnny here in Filey. Will you go and hear him?" She went and was powerfully affected by Johnny's preaching at the evening's service. She invited him back for supper.

After supper, Johnny said to her "Pray a few words, sister." She said "she didn't know how." Johnny said "Now then, ask what thou wants, and believe, only believe." She prayed and she experienced a complete release of all signs of illness. She was made totally well. She was filled with peace and joy and she jumped up off her knees shouting and praising God. The severe depression was gone, never to return.

Her faith remained strong and vibrant right to her death at an advanced age.

She was one of the earliest converts and went on to become one of the key workers in the Filey area helping many people find faith for themselves. She was very effective in raising a great deal of funding both in Filey and London for the Primitive Methodist Society's work. (1)

Johnny would go wherever he was needed. During his visits to the sick, some remarkable cures took place. The case of Elizabeth Ross is one of them. She had been bed bound for seven years. Her condition was described as being:-"the sinews of her knees quite fast, and her legs were stiff and hard, as though they had not a joint in them......quite unable to leave her bed." While in this state Johnny visited her.

After praying with her, he said "thou wilt get better, and be able to walk, for the Lord has told me so. If thou wilt serve the Lord, thou'll never have this affliction again. If thou do not serve Him, it will come to thee again, and thou will never get better any more."

A man, Mr Paddison, had gone with Johnny to see this woman. When Mr Paddison saw Mrs Gordon he said "Johnny has surprised me. He's been praying for Betty Ross and he says she will get better. It's impossible!" Many others also said the same thing when they heard.

However from the day of Johnny's visit, she started to recover. Her joints started to become loose. In a short time she was out of bed, active and strong. She was soon able to run up and down the steep cliff path with a heavy load upon her head like any of the other fishermen's wives. She started going to a place of worship and to live a Christian life.

But she soon began to let go of any faith in Jesus. Later her previous illness returned, she became confined to bed and stayed there for the remainder of her life.

Johnny Oxtoby's words were fulfilled.

As Johnny continued to visit from house to house during the day, and to conduct meetings in the evenings, many of the people became converted.

It is likely, but not recorded, that some experienced people came from Bridlington to help the new converts become established and form The Primitive Methodist Church in Filey. A Chapel was built in Mitford Street to seat 100 people and was in use by the end of 1823.

Some of the early believers became prominent in their own right in the ongoing work in Filey. Local gifted people were recognised and used in preaching and teaching others. At least 25% of the preachers were women. There was no "gender" restriction operating with the Primitive Methodists.

A huge transformation had taken place in the attitudes of the people of Filey in 1823.

One of the most obvious changes was how quickly drunkenness stopped.

Up to March 1823 drunkenness was commonplace. It quickly came to an end when the revival started. During this time alcoholism was a great problem throughout Britain. It was estimated that there were 100,000 alcohol related deaths each year right through the 19th Century. Yet in Filey it stopped almost completely within a very short time.

Other changes were:-

Support given for the Needy

A new spirit of generosity to those in need started. Where previously there had been an almost indifference towards the needy, now there was an unprecedented concern to give help where it was needed. It became normal practice for large sums of money and support to be given out to those experiencing genuine hardship. Money was brought in by various means, collections, some were freewill donations and some other gifts were from giving fish to be sold.

Many of the fishermen, who were Christians, would put out an extra line from their cobles for the work of the Christian cause. All the catch from that line was given for the Lord's work. Voluntary giving in many forms took place. The widows and children of those fishermen who were lost at sea were generously supported. Mariners who were shipwrecked were given lump sums of money to help start them earning again.

The Filey Fishermen's Choir formed

Bawdy tavern singing voices were transformed to be faith filled voices of praise with many of the fishermen becoming staunch Primitive Methodists. They decided that they could and should express their faith through singing. This was the start of the Filey Fishermen's Choir. The choir began travelling through Yorkshire and the North of England, spreading the Good News of God's love through song and their own personal testimony to how the Lord has helped them in times of need. (2)

Filey Fishermen's Choir circa 1930 at Ebenezer Chapel.
Top row, left to right: C Potts (conductor), R Haxby, James Haxby, J Douglas (jnr), F Haxby.
Front row: J W Jenkinson, J Douglas (snr), Rev G Welburn, E Jenkinson, Tom crimlisk.

Coble Landing, Filey circa 1860, prior to the building of the sea wall.
(courtesy of Filey Museum).

Fishermen's work was heavy and laborious before mechanisation, circa 1910
photo. (courtesy Filey Museum).

Filey Fishermen's Choir 2010 at Filey Methodist Chapel

Back row, left to right: David Sheldon (conductor), Raymond Hargrave, Roger Carr, Robert Hall, Don Clark, Ivan Wilkes, Jim Haxby.

Middle row: John Lancaster, Stan Wright, Colin Jowsey, Brian Drake, John Whitehead, Mike Row, Bill Messruther, Francis Appleby (organist).

Front Row: Alan Lumsden, Barry Thompson, Mansfield Atton, Albert Fox, Earnest Sydney.

The Gospel Compass was on permanent display in Ebenezer chapel. Key biblical references were set out as compass points for the church members to steer their lives by. (courtesy of Filey Museum).

The chapel at Muston 2 miles away, was built the following year to John Oxtoby's visit to Filey. This shows the "ripple" effect of the revival going out beyond Filey's boundaries.

Ebenezer Chapel interior decked out for the "Harvest of the Sea Thanksgiving Service" (courtesy of Filey Museum).

Ebenezer Chapel, Union Street, Filey in 2013 now as a housing development.

The Preaching Plan for 1824. John Oxtoby is No 3.
(courtesy Fisher Crimlisk Archives).

John Oxtoby's Grave in Warter Churchyard.

For the "Flither Girls of Filey" – life was particularly tough, as the women had to collect bait as well as run the family home. (courtesy Filey Museum).

Sunday Fishing Stopped

Up to the Revival, Sunday working was normal. However, the new Christian converts were not happy to go on in that way. They saw that Sunday was supposed to be the Lord's Day and not a day for normal working.

The matter was brought to a head when Thomas Cowling refused to take his yawl out to fish on a Sunday. The yawl belonged to an owner at Whitby who had offered to lend it to Thomas for him to use. Thomas accepted the offer, and now that he could choose when he would go out to fish, he immediately decided that he would not go out on Sundays as that was the Lord's Day!

The Jenkinson family also felt the same way. Mr Jenkinson and his three sons, William, John and George decided they would not go out on a Sunday to fish. They bought their own boat and named it "The Three Brothers". They would then be independent of all the others who wanted to fish.

The fishing community divided into two groups over the issue of Sunday fishing.

The pro-working on Sunday group said that the others "waddn't mak a living", they would "sean come ti nowt" and have their boats to sell.

The new converts of Filey prayed that the faith of the no-fishing on Sunday group would be vindicated, and that "their faith would not be disgraced."

When two boats, which had gone out on Saturday night came in with 25,000 herring, there was great rejoicing in the pro-working group. The three brothers were challenged to "git hauf as mich". (get half as much)

The brothers sailed on Monday and came in on Tuesday with 30,000 herring, while their rivals failed to catch anything worthwhile. The brothers sailed on Wednesday and came back again with 30,000. Their rivals had so little fish that they didn't even show up.
On the Thursday they sailed again and the brothers came in with 50,000 herring.
 During that week they had caught 110,000 fish. Their rivals came in with almost nothing. From that time, Sunday fishing was all but finished.

Cobles pulled up on Coble Landing.

There was one more attempt by the pro-Sunday working group to go to sea. When Mrs Gordon, the same Mrs Gordon who had been healed through prayer, met the men going to the boats one Sunday, she tried to persuade them to stay on shore. When they insisted on going, she said "If you go, I'll pray and ask the Lord to send calm and you will not be able to fish today." Nevertheless they went out, and as they entered into the bay, the wind dropped away, and in a dead calm they were unable to fish and had to row home again.

There was no further attempt to go fishing on Sundays for the next 70 years. Even the usual Sunday practice of the skiening (cleaning out shellfish from the shells for bait), baiting and loading the lines for the next day's fishing were abandoned. Amongst the non-Christians it was grudgingly recognised that the Prim fishermen were gaining special favour! There was a proverb which started in Filey that said "If there were only two herrings in the sea, Ranter Jack would be sear (sure) to git yan (one) on em!" Also, "If a ranter went to sea in a wesh-tub (wash-tub) he would come back home wiv mair than onybody else!" (3)

Open Air Services

During the summer months, open air services started to be held on the cliff top. These were very popular and many people gathered together to listen and to speak about their own personal testimony and of their Christian experiences. A feature of their services was the singing of the fishermen.

It became a familiar sound to hear them singing in close harmony, their voices carrying far from the cliff top. Instead of the usual dour and sombre public worship, these times were transformed by joyful singing into a lively happy expression of faith. The people sang heartily of their victory over adversity. The cliff-top "Open Air" services were recorded as still taking place in 1908. J Swane wrote in his diary for Sunday 30 August 1908 – "The fishermen strolled slowly to it" – "the preaching is rough but one of Old Filey's institutions". (4)

New Converts come together as a Church

These different expressions of faith of the Filey folk are reminiscent of the very early church. In the New Testament the early church is described in "The Acts of the Apostles" chapter 2 verses 42-47. This details how the new converts of the day spent their time living their lives and sharing their faith together as they cared for one another powered by the love of God. The very same characteristics were being actively displayed in Filey. The revival had taken the people back to the essential core values of the original church of 1750 years earlier.

As with the early church, the work in Filey was not left to "qualified professional" people outside the community to carry out. Johnny Oxtoby encouraged the new Christians to share *their* faith with those around them, their families, neighbours, and their work-mates. The new converts recognised that it was their responsibility and their privilege to share the good news with those around them. They were simply motivated by love.

They believed and applied the words of Jesus when He answered the question "Which is the most important commandment?" Jesus had replied:-"The most important one is to love the Lord your God with all your heart and with all your soul and with all your mind and with all your strength. The second one is this: Love your neighbour as yourself."(5) The new converts took this message to heart and as they shared their faith, the infant Primitive Methodist Church in Filey rapidly grew in both size and strength.

Some of the local people who took on a prominent role in the work were:-

Mrs Jenkinson, "Nan Jenk", became highly respected because of her strong faith and power in prayer. Her good deeds were influential in helping many people with difficult circumstances in Filey and in the surrounding area. At her death, vast numbers turned out to pay their respects and acknowledge the loss they felt.

Also there was **Mr John Wyvill,** who as a youth, was converted within a couple of days of John Oxtoby's arrival to Filey. Mr Wyvill became one of the mainstays of "The Prims" (Primitive Methodists) work in Filey throughout the whole of his long life. He became a well respected local preacher.

William Jenkinson also was a staunch supporter and member. He died in 1866 but had lived to see more than one hundred of his relatives become members of the Primitive Methodist society.

These are just a few of the many people whose lives which were left as a legacy to build the Church at Filey. They had been transformed through the revival which had begun through the preaching and ministry of John Oxtoby.

Records do not tell us how long Johnny Oxtoby stayed to minister in Filey but he was still in Filey on 23rd April 1823 and so perhaps a little over one month is a fairly good assessment. Because he was so effective in preaching, he was in great demand and was invited to work in many other areas. He is recorded as being appointed to Silsden later in that year of 1823 and to Hull in 1824.

We do know that he was again in Filey in 1824, the Circuit Plan of that year showing him as one of the local preachers to the Filey area.

The Primitive Methodist Society in Filey was now firmly established by this time. Members were commonly known as "Ranters" because of their loud exuberant singing and passionate praying. Theirs was not a quiet hide-in-the-corner type of private faith.

Chapel Building

Excited by their new faith, people wanted to meet and

42

worship together.

In 1824 a new chapel, which they named, "Bethesda", was built in Mitford Street to hold one hundred people. A Sunday school was soon formed. Music was provided by the instruments that had previously been played at taverns and dances, fiddles and melodeons. This was the community expressing its worship 'to make a joyful noise unto the Lord'!

The Prims prospered at Mitford Street and quickly outgrew the original chapel size which had to be extended twice in the next thirty years, to finally be able to hold five hundred people. (6) Not all the new converts joined the Primitives. Some joined with the Methodists and others the Anglicans. God was at work in the people's hearts and all three denominations experienced growth during this period of revival.

For anyone tempted to dismiss this turning to Christianity as mere emotionalism or the response to a particularly gifted orator, it should be noted that the transformation of the community was widespread and long lasting. There was a radical and fundamental change in people's value systems. No longer would they tolerate their old life style. They sought to live their lives to a higher moral and spiritual order.

Faith continued to grow. The Prims numbers continued to increase at Mitford Street and quickly outgrew the original capacity of one hundred seats of Bethesda Chapel. Just nineteen years after the chapel was built it needed to be further extended in 1843. Again only sixteen years later, the congregation had outgrown the extended chapel and a further extension took place in 1859. (6)

As the Prims Church continued to flourish, Mr and Mrs Gordon, John Wyville and William Jenkinson (of "The Three Brothers") grew in prominence and took on various roles of responsibility for the work in Filey.

Mr and Mrs Gordon opened up their home and saw over forty people transformed by God's love and to become established in their faith.

Mrs Gordon was instrumental in the conversion of Ann Cowling, later to become Mrs Jenkinson widely known as "Nan Jenk". Both these women were extremely effective fund raisers.

The amounts that Nan Jenk raised were so consistently large that it was wondered how she managed it. A partial answer at least, was the fact that there was an agreement between the fishermen and her that they would donate a certain percentage of all the fish they caught above a certain quantity to her for the missionary fund, on condition that she prayed for them and their safety while they were fishing.

This arrangement worked well for both parties. (7)

The events that had taken place in the community were quite remarkable, impacting and affecting individuals' lives and the corporate life of the community.

Some of the effects that could be seen were:

- Illnesses, both physical and mental, had been cured through prayer.
- Alcohol addiction cured immediately and permanently. Drunkards becoming good fathers and caring husbands.
- A new spirit of generosity was initiated towards those in great need.
- Bawdy tavern singing voices became faith filled voices and the Filey Fishermen's Choir was formed.
- Lifestyles were changed as shown by the cessation of Sunday fishing.
- People had come together to form a church body and o build a Chapel.
- Numerous individuals had found life-long life changing faith.
- All the above shows that something quite unusual had taken place with the people of Filey.

These changes were not transient, not five day-day-wonders, because they were still evident for at least the next hundred years.

With all these changes coming into the community, Filey felt a much more positive, hopeful and peaceful place to live.

CHAPTER 6:
Faith Tested in the Storm of October 1869.

The community continued to produce men and women of great faith.

The legacy of fishermen with Christian faith continued with Matthew Haxby, the Jenkinson brothers and many others. Their evangelistic work as "the Filey Fishermen" became widely known and they were highly respected because of their personal integrity, their solid consistency and their reliability. They were influential to many.

Their faith was not a weak, wimpish "Sunday only" faith! Their faith was gritty, gutsy, resilient and real. It was what made them who they were. Their faith went to sea with them as they went fishing. It was the resilient force which enabled them to face, with confidence, the risks which went with that hazardous way of life in the days of sail. This is best seen in the events which occurred the autumn of 1869. Unbeknown to them, Monday the 25th of October was the beginning of the Great Storm of 1869 which hit the East Coast of England with tremendous ferocity.

On Monday the 25th October, thirty-one yawls belonging to Filey left Scarborough harbour, along with fifty five vessels belonging to Scarborough, and sailed east by north-east until they reached the fishing ground about thirty miles out from land.

Very soon the wind began to blow increasing strongly until in a short time it rose to gale force. The gale continued to grow in intensity over the next three days with mountainous seas and shrieking winds which delivered snow, frost, thunder and lightning to the vulnerable seamen.

On the Thursday 28th, over the storm Matthew Haxby, who was a local preacher, shouted out Psalm 77, and then with the crew, sang five verses of the hymn "Jesus lover of my soul, let me to thy bosom fly." He had insisted that he should be lashed to the tiller, and then he steered the vessel for most of the seventy hours, because, he said, "If a wave washes me overboard, I am alright. I shall go straight to heaven, where there is no more sea."

Mr Matthew Haxby.

Richard Haxby senior, similarly said to his crew, "Now, some of you have a wife and young children dependent upon you; I have a wife that I well prize, but no young children, therefore you should seek every precaution to shun risk and escape death. Besides, you are not ready for another world. Frank and I are insured for eternal life, therefore lash us to the tiller and you go below where there is less danger."

Confident of God's love for them, they were prepared to lay down their lives for those around them. That was their faith in action.

George Jenkinson, local preacher and skipper of "The Good Intent" recorded his experience.

He said "On Tuesday, the waves were of mountainous size and very threatening. We prayed for help and the Lord heard us. By the evening there were the signs of the storm increasing in ferocity and we asked the Lord to stretch forth His mighty hand, through the night, on our behalf. Our hearts were ready to fail us. But the Lord was greater than our hearts, He sustained us.

At this time I found the Lord very powerfully present, and, addressing the men, I said, "The best thing that all of you can do is to prepare for another state of existence – that is, for heaven. Jesus says, 'I am the resurrection and the life; and he that believeth in me though he were dead, yet shall he live; and whosoever liveth and believeth in me shall never die'

On Thursday morning, the wind and waves continuing violent,

I earnestly prayed that the Lord would send deliverance, and ventured to believe that He would do so, according to His promise made to the prayer of faith. In the afternoon one of the men John Richardson asked me what I thought to our being saved. I replied, 'I believe we shall be saved.'" (1)

On Thursday, Jenkinson Haxby, local Preacher and skipper of "The Felicity" said to the rest of the crew, "I think we have done all we can to secure our safety, but the gale abates nothing, and there seems but little probability of our getting home any more; the best thing each one can do now is to seek a full preparation for another world."
However on day four, the storm abated, calm gradually ensued and the boats reached home safely on the 30th October.

Mr Jenkinson Haxby.

There were eighty six fishing vessels out at sea from Scarborough and Filey. The thirty-one vessels which went out from Filey had on board three hundred lives, men and boys. They lost virtually all their fishing tackle. The loss was estimated to be £8,000.(2) That not one life was lost was considered miraculous protection. On reaching home one young man said to his mother, *"I knew you were praying for me."*

FILEY.

THE LATE GALE.——Never within the memory of the oldest fishermen was a gale known to last so long as that which has just swept along the coast. The hurricane of wind, accompanied with blinding sleet and snow—the sea lashed into fury, with its wave upon wave like mountains, rolling and roaring like peal after peal of thunder as they broke upon the rocky beach—and, knowing that 22 yawls, manned by 300 human beings, belonging to Filey, would be battling with the elements in all their fury, created such intense anxiety and produced such a gloom and melancholy foreboding, as, perhaps, was never witnessed in Filey before. From morning till night, the telegraph-office was besieged by anxious wives, mothers, and children, hoping to hear good news from some port or other; and all through the night they paced the streets to the cliff, to gaze upon the terrific sea. After days of suspense, news came of the safety of first one and then another, until (as by a miracle) all were heard of, but with the loss of all their nets, warps, and barrels, a loss that cannot be estimated at less than £8,000. The tales told of hair-breadth escapes, the cries and tears of the poor fellows as the engulphing waves broke over them, are thrilling in the extreme. Devotional thanksgiving services for their great deliverence were held last Sunday in both the Wesleyan and Primitive chapels, which were well attended.

The Filey News published the report of the 1870 Storm
(courtesy Fisher Crimlisk Archives).

Yet at the same time three Scarborough yawls, the "Prosperity", "Rambler" and the "John Wesley" were lost with all thirty one men on board. Because of this, fourteen Scarborough wives lost their husbands and 25 children their fathers.(2) Similarly, there was a great loss of life amongst the fishermen of Yarmouth.

It was estimated that 860 people lost employment in the Filey and Scarborough locality, at least temporarily; through the effects of the storm. (2)

This compounded the economic hardship for many families. Their plight, as a result of the storm, was publicised in various newspapers and so became widely known. This resulted in public meetings being held in several towns including Scarborough, Driffield and as far distant as Sheffield to collect donations for those affected.

To the Editor of the Driffield Times.

Sir,—May we request of you the great favour of opening your columns to the following case of extreme distress in Filey, consequent on the severe and protracted gales of last week? The calamity which has befallen the fishermen is altogether unparalleled in the memory of the oldest inhabitant in this village. The loss in fishing-nets alone belonging to working fishermen is estimated about £8,000. The fishermen have lost all their means on which they are entirely dependent for their bread, and, unless prompt assistance can be obtained, the most dreary and heartrending prospect awaits them and their families. They are literally stripped of the means of subsistence and are incapable of turning themselves to any other calling. Filey will not be able to recover itself for very many years if left to itself, as there are very few persons of independent means among its resident inhabitants; so that, unless considerable assistance is obtained from extraneous sources a fine race of men will be prostrated, disheartened, and ruined in this world. We earnestly hope and trust that many who are acquainted with Filey as a favourite-watering-place may be induced to compassionate the poor fishermen in their present appalling calamity. Subscriptions will be thankfully received by any of us, who beg to subscribe ourselves yours, most faithfully,

     T. N. JACKSON, Vicar of Filey for 36 years.
     JOHN UNITT, of Filey and Edgbaston.
     ARTHUR PETTITT, Curate of Filey.
     R. W. ALLEN, Wesleyan Minister.
     C. KENDALL, P.M. Minister.
     ROBERT CAMMISH, Merchant.

Filey, Nov. 1.

After the storm of 1870 an appeal for financial support for the fishermen of Filey was published in The Driffield Times. Their need became widely known, some contributions came in from Sheffield.

The Filey fishermen said that their survival was clearly due to Divine protection. They recognised that the Lord had protected them and they readily proclaimed it as such.

Jenkinson Haxby went on to faithfully serve with the Primitive Methodists for the rest of his life. He was highly respected and was honoured in 1902 by being made a Permanent Member of the Primitive Methodist Conference.

Chapter 7:
Building for the Future.

The Primitive Methodists continued to prosper. Numbers continued to increase. The local newspaper, The Filey Post stated on 11th January 1867 "--although 'Bethesda' chapel had been enlarged twice since it opened in 1823, the 600 people's capacity is now too small."

Even though six hundred could be accommodated, it was still not possible for all the families to be able to sit together in family groups. The members could see that a new building was needed.

At a Leaders meeting on 20th November 1865 it was decided that this had to be addressed and a new building begun. This was the birth of the new venture, the building of "Ebenezer" Chapel. It was decided that there would be a 'Halibut Supper' at the end of the Spring fishing season in 1866. This would be the start of the Chapel building fund.
21st September 1867 saw the decision officially taken that a new Chapel should be built, and that it must be capable of seating *seven hundred* people.

A site was found that was suitable on Union Street and permission was given to Rev Parkinson Milson, Mr Bulmer and Mr Milner to look to buy it for no more than £400. This was done and 1868 saw the project moving forward.

Bricks would be needed. In fact two hundred thousand bricks were needed to build not only the Chapel but also a suitable house for the Minister and his family.

Daniel Deeton successfully tendered for the job of making bricks with the price of ten shillings and eleven pence (approx 55p in modern terms) per thousand bricks.

The clay from the site was to be used for the bricks. The year 1869 started with high hopes.

Fund raising activities proceeded with a Bazaar and a public tea on Good Friday. At the March Quarterly Meeting a board of Trustees was formed for the new Chapel. The new Trustees sanctioned "the erection of a Chapel at Filey to seat seven hundred and fifty persons, the entire cost of which must not exceed £2500."

Finances were slower to come in than anticipated. By June 1869, the project was starting to run into difficulty. There was a large deficit. Special collections were needed but still there was a shortage.

Throughout the country the majority of the Primitive Methodists were financially poor people. It was the manual labourers, the ordinary housewives, the maids and the people with the lower paid jobs, who made up the vast bulk of the Primitives' congregations.

As a consequence, their faith for building a new chapel was usually greater than their available funds. This was normal. At other locations Primitive Methodist Chapels usually had debts for the initial building work.

The availability of funds did not dictate whether a chapel was built. Faith was such that they believed that the Lord would supply the shortfall. If they were doing the right thing then the Lord would provide!

Eventually, at Filey, individual members generously made up the shortfall. In the Treasurer's report, is written "Deficiency made up by a few friends whose reward is on high". (1) Many ordinary people gave to the fund as they were able and without regard of their own needs.

A resident of Filey, recently recalled to the author-: "My great grandmother gave her last five pounds to the building fund." As a comparison, twelve pounds plus board and lodging was the hiring rate for *the year* for a man working on farms at that time. So five pounds really was sacrificial giving as it represented several months' wages! Yet it was typical of many similar gifts.

At Filey the difficulties with the finances in June were multiplied by the events of the great storm of October of that year. While none of the fishermen were lost, the great depletion of so much of their fishing gear left many of them with great problems. It was reckoned that £8000 worth of tackle was lost between them. This was a devastating cost to the community.

So, although two hundred thousand bricks were ready, the actual start of building had to be postponed. The many piles of bricks were left lying there on site waiting for sufficient funds to be gathered so that work on the chapel could be started. The fishermen continued to support the building of the chapel as soon as they were able. Some gave whole catches from some of their nets; others dedicated certain lines to the fund.

Eventually, on 5th July 1870 the foundation stone was laid by Mrs Ellis from Grimsby. She was the director of a large timber merchants' company and after being much impressed by the singing of the Filey fisherman, she donated all the pitch pine timber which was needed for the building of the Chapel.

The new Chapel was opened 18th June 1871, and as an act of dedication, it was decided to ask for 'golden collections', half-sovereigns and sovereigns only. This again was sacrificial giving and was only achieved with wholehearted support for the cause by many committed people. The chapel opened for the first Sunday Service was on 22nd June 1871 with great rejoicing and much celebration! The "Prims" finally had their new place of worship--"Ebenezer"--The Fishermen's Chapel!

Ebeneezer Chapel newly built 1870. (courtesy of Filey Museum).

Many fishermen were used as Lay Preachers. Their simple, powerful preaching resonated well with the congregation, their shared knowledge of the trials, the uncertainties and experiences of being fishermen gave their message both relevancy and an immediacy with which the congregation could identify.

Sometimes their enthusiasm outweighed accuracy as was the

case when a Lay Preacher was preaching on Isaiah 60 v2 "Gross darkness covered the people". The preacher asked the people "Do you know what gross darkness is?" Then he thundered the answer, "I'll tell you what gross darkness is! It's a hunded and fotty fower darknesses, that's what gross darkness is!" (a gross was an old measure for 12 dozen i.e. 12x12 =144).

At Ebenezer, the people could identify with, and understand, the local broad Yorkshire language of the preachers and the colloquialisms that they used. This contrasted sharply with some of the sermons of the older established churches. Soon the singing of the congregation became widely known and many visitors came to these services and commented on how they had been inspired and encouraged by being there. Such had been the need for the building that it was frequently in use every day of the week, particularly in the evenings with bible studies and prayer meetings for whatever needs that there were.

The building of "Ebenezer Chapel", with a seating capacity of over seven hundred people, is clear evidence for the huge transformation which had taken place in the population's spiritual life between 1823 and 1871. The contrast between the previous old Filey community attitudes with that of the new life, is so distinct that the changes can only be described as quite remarkable.

Up until 1823 people had rejected virtually everything

to do with Christianity. By 1865 there was a need for a place of worship which could hold seven hundred in addition to the premises of the other church denominations.

The 1871 census figure for Filey shows the population as being 2267. Yet seven hundred seats were still needed in addition to the seating for the other congregations in the town. This was an enormously high number of seats for a population figure of this size. There were enough seats available to cater for half the population at any one time!

A tremendous change had come over Filey in the relatively short time of less than forty two years. The resulting transformation of the life of the town was so profound that it caused much outside interest and books were published which described the remarkable turnaround of the people's value system and their subsequent behaviour.

It wasn't so much that they had changed their behaviour so that they *could be loved* by God, but rather their behaviour had changed because they knew that they *were loved* by God. Faith had initially sprung into being through the preaching of Johnny Oxtoby. Faith continued to flow down through many families and many generations.

In February 2013 the author had the privilege of talking with Jim Haxby, a resident of Filey. Jim is a descendant of the same family who were so closely associated with the early

Prims, being the great- grandson of Matthew Haxby, the same Matthew Haxby whose testimony is recounted in chapter 6 of this book 'Faith tested in the Storm of October 1869'. As Jim talked about his working life at sea, it was apparent that the rich seam of faith is still present and active in today's generation of the Haxby family.

He described how on one occasion he could so nearly have come to disaster. He said that his brother Dick, together with himself and his son James went out fishing in their coble against his brother's wishes. His brother had felt that the sea was too rough and that they shouldn't go out. But Jim thought otherwise and persuaded him that it would be alright and against his brother's better judgement, they put out to sea.

But once they were well out into the bay it was much rougher than Jim had anticipated. There were huge seas running with big waves breaking all around them. They realised then that they had made a big mistake. It wasn't safe to keep going. They turned back towards Filey, but there were huge waves breaking both behind the coble and also breaking in front of them.

But, Jim said, the amazing thing was that on the way back their boat was always in a place of relative calm. They noticed that the huge waves were continually breaking behind them and also in front of them. But where they were was always clear of the big breakers. He said that it was not a natural calm;

he said "I know that it was the Lord who was making the sea calm for us to get home". And it continued like that all the way back, allowing them to return safely to shore, very relieved and very thankful! Jim said that they knew that there had been a helping hand to get them back to shore.

The Filey Fishermen's Choir is still active today in 2013. The same basic principles are still in place now as they were at the choir's initial inception. Their programme is varied but always includes their personal expression of their Christian faith. The programme typically is a mixture of hymns and other spiritual songs interspersed with personal testimony. Jim Haxby is an active member of The Filey Fishermen's Choir and is now in his 53rd year as a member.

Subsequently the choir has appeared several times on national television and has sung on numerous international stages. The choir has always remained faithful to its original fishing roots by continuing to wear the unique navy-blue Filey 'gansey' as they give public performances. The choir continues to be active today after only a short break enforced by the war years. Their website page clearly and boldly testifies that the choir was originally formed in 1823 and due directly to the ministry of Johnny Oxtoby.

Jim went on to explain to the author about how their experiences at sea were often used by the individual members of the choir. In their testimonies they often speak of the situations and difficulties that they have encountered.

For example, he said, at sea a northerly gale was very difficult for getting back into Filey. It was the worst direction for the wind to come from, the seas being violent and difficult to steer through.

Yet once through into the bay and inside Filey Brigg then there is always calm water! This illustration is sometimes used for the choir to then sing "Shelter from the Storm" which describes how the Lord is always similarly able to give shelter to us from the storms of life's experiences.

It is good to know that the light of faith is still shining through the ministry of The Filey Fishermen's Choir even after the intervening period of 190 years.

In conclusion, we can see that late March 1823 was the start of a quite remarkable period of history. Here we see all the hallmarks of a spiritual revival taking place. It was a revival that only came about because heaven reached down and touched Filey. For many people at Filey, the experience of this heavenly touch was deeply personal, being both profound and permanently life changing.

Chapter 8:

The Filey Revival and the Challenges for today.

The preceding pages may give rise to some questions which need answers:-

What is meant by the term "Revival"?

When we use the name "revival" we are describing a move of the Holy Spirit which reveals God's love and His holiness to people who have previously had little awareness of God.

This heavenly initiative brings people to an awareness of their need for God. It brings a *personal* awareness of one's own need, of one's intrinsic poverty, a poverty which is unrelated to status, financial wealth, relationships or possessions.

The Christian author Colin Whittaker describes it as *"one of those special seasons of Divine visitation when God the Holy Spirit quickens and stirs up the slumbering church."* (1)

This results in people urgently desiring to know more of God and to seek to draw closer to God. They are drawn to study the bible, to pray and meet together with others who are similarly moved. There is a great awareness of God's holiness, His purity and his immense love for them. *"----the most hardened and sceptical are brought under conviction of sin, leading to genuine repentance and saving faith in the Lord Jesus Christ---."* (1)

This happened to the people of Filey in 1823 and continued until at least 1870 and probably well beyond. The Filey revival was part of a great movement of spiritual awakening in the period 1804-1830.

During this period it was the Primitive Methodist Church that was used as a catalyst for revival to sweep through many communities. Research shows that the neighbouring towns of Bridlington, Scarborough, Flamborough and the surrounding villages were also powerfully affected. Many other towns and villages across the Midlands and North of England also encountered this powerful revival experience.(2)

The Primitive Methodists were extremely effective in bringing the Gospel to the ordinary working people as they spoke a simple language that the people could readily relate to and appreciate. Their message was simple but it was not just a message given by the efforts of people. It was endued with the essential power that originates in heaven.

Revival broke out, as in Filey, in Weardale (Durham) when Johnny Oxtoby moved there. Revival swept the full length of that valley also.

When true revival breaks out it is always the work of God. No human agency can make it happen. Yet usually there is some human involvement.

God does use naturally gifted people, but He also uses

ordinary folk to show that regeneration is the work of the Holy Spirit and is not dependant on human abilities.

Johnny Oxtoby was such a man. He had little education and no natural eloquence. His mental abilities were considered to be "unremarkable". In stature and bearing he was unimpressive, his language was not considered "respectable" because of his broad "uncouth" Yorkshire accent.

But one thing he had in abundance was that he had great faith. He was a man of prayer, and God's strength, which comes through prayer, enabled Oxtoby to be used effectively from 1823 to when he left this world to be with his Lord in 1830. (3)

There have been many revivals over the past centuries, when very ordinary people have been used by God in revival work to transform communities.

The Filey Revival of 1823 came to an almost godless town where human depravity went virtually unchecked.

The community where the Church was struggling to survive changed to a town that was clamouring for bigger premises to cater for those wanting to worship!

From Godlessness to Godliness! What a change!

Such changes can only come about by Revival Power – "power from on high."

OXTOBY'S GRAVE.

Photograph copied from
"The Origin and History of the Primitive Methodist Church"
by H. B. Kendall

How long did the Filey Revival last?

Nationally, 'The Ranters Revival' is generally considered to have been from 1804 to 1830.(4) However there is evidence that it continued much longer at Filey. Rev Parkinson Milson's diary entry for 27 January 1868 reads, *"We have a Revival here. One saved at Staxton, three at Gristhorpe, eighteen at Hunmanby, ten at Muston, sixteen at Filey"*.

20ᵗʰ March 1868 *".........we have over one hundred converted this last year, we have now three hundred members in Filey ......"*

The demand for extra seating in places of Christian worship is a good indicator of Revival life. The need for the new Chapel gives added proof of the continuing growth of numbers of young people becoming members of the Church. Many others attended who were not officially members but viewed Ebenezer as "their" Chapel. Hence the need for seven hundred extra seats.

It is safe to conclude that the Revival at Filey lasted from March 1823 to at least 1870 and probably well beyond.

Why did the Revival end?

If we compare the "impetus" of Revival to that of, say, the energy needed for a train to travel on a level railway track, we can see a similar dynamic operating within Revival.

If the train has accelerated from being stationary, to say, 100 mph, the increase in speed has been obvious to all. Energy, in whatever form, electricity, diesel or steam has powered it and given it <u>momentum</u> i.e. the ability to move.

If the power is withdrawn the **momentum** will still carry the train forward. The drop in speed will be gradual and at first unnoticed. From 100mph to 90mph the change will be imperceptible.

It is still travelling at 90mph compared to previously being stationary. But the train is slowing and will eventually stop, because of the lack of fresh energy being given.

Revival is very similar. The energy for revival is always from the Lord. It is the power of God which causes it, energises it and sustains it.

If for any reason He withdraws from the work, and only the <u>momentum</u> remains, then the work will lose the freshness, the vitality and the sense of the Lord's presence, which was originally present when the revival started. Men's effort cannot sustain the revival.

Revival causes people to come to the Lord. They come to Him desperately aware of their deepest need – which is to come to have a close and surrendered relationship with Jesus. For each it is a <u>personal</u> experience.

The experience of one generation cannot ever be fully handed down to the next.

Just hearing about something, however profound it may be, can never have the same impact as actually experiencing that life-changing event personally.

Describing an experience to someone is not the same as the person experiencing the event. People, who have been transformed through the revival process, are *changed* people.

As that generation aged and then died out, the next generation after the revival often only had second-hand experiences to sustain them. So the momentum slowed down.

As this happens, frequently 'legalism' comes in and emphasises the negative, the "do nots" (i.e. *do not* go dancing, attending cinemas, drinking alcohol, smoking, gambling etc) and it is the negatives that tends to replace the previous emphasis on holiness and the need for salvation.

Hard work alone cannot sustain revival. Eventually the Primitive Methodist Church was unable to sustain the work. This resulted in the Primitive Methodists uniting with the Wesleyan Methodists and the United Methodists in 1932.

Ebenezer Chapel closed in 1975 and subsequently became a housing development in 2006.

If Revival happened in the community where I live, what would be the effect on everyday life that I would see?

When the power of God falls on a place the people there are very aware of it.

It causes ordinary people to want to get their lives straightened out and to live their lives to God's standards. We can see from past revivals how changes have been quite dramatic and much of society's values have been turned upside down.

The Welsh Revival of 1904-1905 is well documented.(5)

There we see enormous changes taking place. Some of them are listed below.

- Crime figures dropping so dramatically that the Magistrates had few cases to try.
- Hardened unbelievers converted (becoming Christians).
- Alcohol and gambling addicts getting set free of their addictions.
- Pubs being almost deserted, some going out of business for lack of trade

[at this time approx 100,000 people died each year in Britain through alcohol related deaths.]

- Old debts re-paid.
- Prayer Meetings crowded.
- Coal miners holding prayer meetings before going down the mines.
- Pit ponies having to be re-trained because they couldn't obey the cleaned up language and behaviour of the miners. Previously the ponies were cursed and kicked into working.
- In two years over 100,000 outsiders converted and flocked to join Church congregations.

When revival comes, the effect is to halt social, moral and spiritual decay. Many would agree that today's society in the UK shows much evidence of decay in social, moral and spiritual values.

With UK prisons overcrowded, soaring crime rates, with drug and alcohol addiction at high and still escalating levels, promiscuity widespread and the increasing need for CCTV cameras to combat anti-social behaviour – all indicate that society in the UK has problems which are in urgent need of addressing.

When revival does happen again, we will see many of our social, moral and spiritual problems reduced and the trends will be reversed.

- Crime rates will fall
- City streets will become safe, night or day
- Pornography will loose its hold and be shunned
- TV programmes will be wholesome and without offensive language or behaviour
- Abortion rates will dramatically fall
- Marriage will become highly valued again
- Traditional family life will be restored and valued
- Addicts of all types will be able to get free from their addictions
- People will care for one another practically
- Senior Citizens will be honoured and respected

- Young people will have vision, energy and a sense of belonging
- Church congregations will grow in size because people will want to "worship in spirit and truth"

There have been "Revivals" or "Awakenings" taking place in many areas of the world throughout the centuries on numerous occasions. Some examples that have taken place in the British Isles in the last 150 years are listed below.

Period

1957 – 58   North Uist Revival - See "When God came Down", by John Ferguson (ISBN 09514997X).

John Ferguson was the Church of Scotland Minister at Portree, Isle of Skye, where the author and he met. He said that when he was a young man he was on North Uist and personally witnessed the revival and was greatly influenced by it.

1949 – 53   Lewis & Harris Revival

1939   Lewis Revival

1920– 21   East Scotland (Fraserburgh, Dundee, Aberdeen, Wick, Thurso)

1904– 06   The Welsh Revival - See "The Welsh Revival of 1904" by Eifion Evans

1859 – 60   The British Revival – This was widespread and on a massive scale. It swept through the whole of Britain.

In Scotland 300,000 people joined the Church during

these two years, 1859-60 i.e. 10% of the entire population of 3,000,000.

Many other examples could be listed, but it is outside the scope of this work to do so.

An intriguing question to close with is:-

(5) Could 'Revival' happen again in this generation in my community?

We need to bear in mind that the Bible tells us that "God is the same yesterday, today and for ever" (Hebrews chapter 13 verse 8) and also that the basic human need is still the same now as it has always been.

It has been said that "the real heart of the human problem is the problem of the human heart." Which tells us that despite much improvement for our comfort and the conveniences of our modern lifestyle; basically we still have exactly the same needs as previous generations.

Can Revival happen again? Well, why not? It has happened before!

There is a fascinating promise in the Bible, where God is speaking in the passage 2 Chronicles Chapter 7 verse 14. The whole verse reads "......*If my people who are called by my name will humble themselves and pray and seek my face and turn from their wicked ways, then will I hear from heaven and will forgive their sin and will heal their land."* (New International Version of the Bible)

What the Lord is saying through this is that if his people, just ordinary believers, will fulfil the four conditions of humbling/praying/seeking/turning, then **HE** will then act and fulfil the rest which includes **HIS PROMISE** "to heal the land."

That is precisely what happened in Filey in 1823.
If the committed Church of today really desires to see a healing of the ills of our present day society, then the keys shown in this scripture need to be applied.

Then we can expect the promise to be fulfilled, because it is a promise from God.

Johnny Oxtoby frequently said **"Only pray and believe, only pray and believe, *then* you will see great things!"** That was his testimony; could it also be ours for today?

Bibliography

Much of the material has been obtained from "The Life of John Oxtoby—(Praying Johnny)" -Rev George Shaw, first published 1894, reprinted 2002.

Chapter 1

1. p102-"The Origin and History of the Primitive Methodist Church"-HB Kendall 1906
2. p 40 "Yorkshire Fisherfolk" -Peter Frank
3. p7- "Shipwrecks of the Yorkshire Coast"- Arthur Godfrey and Peter J Lessey.
4. "Scarborough Herald" Newspaper 26th September 1839.

Chapter 2

1. "History"- Petty
2. p 45 "Great Revivals"- Colin Whittaker.
3. "Wesley's Journals" –John Wesley
4. p 102 "The Origin and History of the Primitive Methodist Church" – HB Kendall.
5. "Filey:-A Yorkshire Fishing Town"- Irene E Allen and Andrew A Todd.
6. "Our Filey Fishermen"-Rev George Shaw

Chapter 3

1. "You must be born again"- The words of Jesus-John Ch3 v3 The Bible. (New International Version)

2. "Primitive Methodism on the Yorkshire Wolds"-Woodcock

Chapter 4

1. James Chapter 5 verse 16b- The Bible (NIV)
2. Fruit of the Spirit- Galatians chapter 5 verse 22. The Bible. (NIV)
3. "Our Filey Fishermen" – Rev George Shaw 1867
4. "You shall receive Power from on High"- The word's of Jesus. Acts Chapter 1 verse 8   The Bible. (New King James Version)
5. p37 " Life of John Oxtoby"-Rev G Shaw 1894
6. Acts Chapters 2, 3 and 4. The Bible (all versions)

Chapter 5

1. "Life of Johnny Oxtoby"- Rev G Shaw.
2. See   Filey   Fishermen's   Choir   website   www. thefileyfishermenschoir.co.uk
3. p83 "Filey- A Yorkshire Fishing Town"- Irene E Allen and Andrew A Todd.
4. P85. Ditto.
5. Matthew Ch5 verses37-38.-The Bible (NIV)
6. "Filey Ebenezer 1871-1971"- F Hanson
7. p81 "Filey-A Yorkshire fishing Town"- Irene E Allen and Andrew A Todd.

Chapter 6.

The major part of this chapter is based on Kendall's book "God's Hand in the Storm" 1870. This was the most complete account that I could find. It was the most topical and personal account, being written and printed within only a few months of the events of the storm and the accounts were given by eye-witnesses with the details still fresh in their memories. AB.

1. p23 "God's Hand in the Storm" –C Kendall 1870.
2. The Filey Post Newspaper 6th November 1869
3. Scarborough Mercury 5th November 1869.

Chapter 7

The source of most of the information for this chapter is from F Hanson's book "Filey Ebenezer 1871-1971." This is a thorough account and record of the Chapel's development. AB.

1. p4 "Filey Ebenezer 1871-1971" – F Hanson.

Chapter 8
1. p21 "Great Revivals"- Colin Whittaker 1984 Marshall Pickering
2. p102 "The Origin and History of the Primitive Methodist Church"- H B Kendall 1906-07.
3. p120 "Life of John Oxtoby" Rev G Shaw (2002 Reprint)
4. p56 "Great Revivals"- Colin Whittaker
5. p 89-97 "Great Revivals"-Colin Whittaker.

A final word: -

If in reading the story of the revival at Filey you feel that you would like to find out more for yourself about the reality of the Christian faith, there are various steps that you can take. The "Alpha Course" from Holy Trinity Brompton (HTB) is one of the excellent tools available.

It is widely advertised by participating churches and has helped many people of all ages. The HTB website will provide the links. Alternatively, if the Alpha Course is not readily available, the author can recommend other material if required. The author can be contacted through email: alanbot32@gmail.com.